Descent & Other Poems

Timothy Ogene

DEERBROOK EDITIONS

PUBLISHED BY
Deerbrook Editions
P.O. Box 542
Cumberland, ME 04021
www.deerbrookeditions.com
www.issuu.com/deerbrookeditions

FIRST EDITION

© 2016 by Timothy Ogene
All rights reserved

ISBN: 978-0-9975051-0-8

On the cover: Artwork by Clare MacKenzie

Book design by Jeffrey Haste

Contents

December	11
Erratic Notes Left on a Trail	12
Sub-surface Conditions	29
Descent	34
As it is Elsewhere	41
Lost Voice	42
Displacement	43
Cassava	44
A Small Experiment	49
Supplication	51
From Cradle to Puzzles	52
Kru Child	53
Above a Postwar Town	54
Boy in Transition	55
Notes to Note	56
Transition	57
Life on a Bamboo Shelf	58
Holes Filled with Mud	59
A Whisper, A Chime	60
Gunpowder	64
A Pinch to the Skin	66

For Clare

The first apple is beginning its descent.

All I know is that years from now, when its glistening torso rolls across these cobblestones, no children will come out to greet it.

—John Yau, "The Pleasures of Exile"

December

An empty bench in the open, frosted over,
A naked tree pregnant with time stuffed
In its widening trunk, boughs bent by icicles
Bunched like chandeliers on winter's x-axis;

A river exiled from its state,
Currents curtailed at both terminals,
Rendered dry after much hammering
In winter's metal works.

In the view ahead,
Gothic structures argue with skylines
Bored by the absence of be-goggled oglers.

There's beauty here, I say to myself,
In this isolated patch stripped of the stench
Of gutters after a downpour.

There is a type of beauty here,
In this absence of motion,
This giddy absence of flirtatious fruits on trees,

In this glorious absence of paraded Polaroid
Swung as crumbs are hauled at native ducks,

In this relieving absence of poachers
Making passes at passengers on the same tour.

There is beauty in absence,
When trees,
Holding time in absent leaves,
Await winter's worst
And the delayed return of summer.

Erratic Notes Left on a Trail

1

A bridge emerges from the remains of fog,
Imposing itself on my sight.

Its arch beautifully humped,
And I'm reminded of lumps on cow back,

The meaty spot a murderous blade
Must be thrilled to hack.

Underneath the bridge the river ebbs
And murmurs

As it journeys with a terminus in mind,
An infinite end

Albeit sure to empty
And rethread the loop.

A clearer view.
A carpet of algae wraps the bridge,

Draining its prehistoric strength,
Probing its intestines with roots we wish we had.

2

For those we love
We refrain from easy paths

And restrain the
Urge to run.

3

A note written in fog, on clear glass
Is memory erased at noon;

Falling and dipping in love
Left to fade in the face of light.

4

Home is where the umbilical chord lies
Buried between gnarled shrubs half-dead,

Overgrown and coated in shame,
A lie too crass to smear.

5

A dog follows its owner over the river,
Across the algae-covered bridge,
To the stare of sailing ducks.

May we return as geese and sailing ducks:
Humble, instinctual, without the tact
To shell schools elsewhere,
To click the tongue at the remains of others.

6

The landscape is an apparition of a master's piece
Discarded, rediscovered to great acclaim:
Fields of gold-colored leaves in fourteen stations of death
Lie to give depth, individually crisp,
The sky defaced with V-shaped strokes
Left for critics to name as birds.

There's a swoosh of blue turning green,
An illusion of a nearby sea,
And ducks paddling between surfaces,
Sailing towards the sun in salutation,
Sailing towards a perennial ritual,
To a ritual that tethers us against our will.

7

I see a girl running up the bridge.
Her polyester coat makes a sideway sweep
Against the wind.
A guardian in fur follows from behind,
Her eyes on the young.

Our girl has crossed the bridge,
And calls the fur to make real haste.
The fur has stopped to stare,
Holding the journey to a halt,
Holding the future to an ambivalent past.

8

A tear is heavier than a severed leaf,
A sigh lighter than the crash of cymbals.

When asked my home address,
I respond with a sigh,
And watch severed leaves land on dormant grounds.

9

I left without a lover's smell in my hair,
Without memories of my mother's hug.
The passage home is burnt and that I regret.

10

A kiss recalled is adolescence restored,
Life remounted for another flight.

Amnesia is the burden of growth,
Of which I am a square instance.

Memory is a pinch and not the whole,
An aftertaste without a meal.

I remember the tongue and not the kiss,
The resistance of breasts and not the hug.

So I write this day in fog,
Knowing it will fade to not return.

11

Dear Mother, it's another day here,
Another night, I mean to say.

It's a dance of darkness, Mother,
And it takes two to do the bleak waltz,

Hips grinding blindly, legs leisurely shuffling
Until sweat breaks forth;

Until the cheer of gloom, the shrouded daylight,
Is shredded in forgettable bits.

12

May this silence unease you, Mother,
May those absent calls,

The phone hanging obese on the wall,
Unease you.

But I prefer this to a thousand funerals.
Or which is best, Mother?

This, or the confused colors
Of spiteful mourners?

13

I come from a place where roads lead nowhere, to graves,
The wind an impractical joke that blows askance,
Rising from the soles of our feet,

Uprooting us before our first human steps;
Where children run homes and plough the fields,
And dogs walk the living through death's orchard.

These we mention in passing:
At the wedding of a thrice-removed niece,
At a dance for abandoned gods.

The world hangs by the toes, dangling,
And its head bulges with blood, a burst as imminent
As the next shot in daylight.

14

We are told he stopped at twenty-one,
Our Rimbaud, having gathered what we all envy.
Then he left his home and invaded mine,
That adventurer I begrudge not.

Ash and Ashbery shared a stand,
Catalogued and shelved as one,
A minor logistic that assumed significance
As I hunted the latter but fell for both,

A treat I shindiged with a loud sucking
Of Turkish delight, recontexting
Myself in Ash's words:

"Think of yourself as open. Equally hard.
Usually your gestures seem to take place
[Behind] a glass partition, fogged with steam."

15

A pony is purchased for a lad who hasn't said a word
Since his tongue lay itself for normal speech.

I see him galloping through green earth,
His smile a cover for speech,

His dimples as deep as mine.
But here's the deal as I am told:

Dreams are embers in a December night,
Dying into senseless flakes at the hearth,

Useless save the past they paint while we sleep.
The coloring is grim and dire at times:

Constipated nights and all,
A peristaltic push and passage painfully stopped,

The hinds of a horse stuck to a haunted carriage,
And dawn dispiritingly delayed.

16

"I have a lover of flesh," Day Lewis says.
Mine used to be fresh, I say, but is now no more,
A country with boundaries made of straw,
A loveless sprawl dispersed by the wind,
Her seeds sprinkled away for birds to pick.

There is a Whitman in everyone, I say.
Rebellion relies on language, I say,
And so does a joke that falls on all,
Including the bystander whose isolation
Is geographic and linguistic.

Power resides in the pinny of a maid:
Fanon in the polish of the master's shoe,
Foucault in the politics of his son's stare.
They will survive this flare,
And the boil will blister into a new brew,

For a stone tossed in a lake must be left to tumble down
To the bottom, and there, patted by currents,
It will fathom its float to shore,
Or waltz its way to a safe corner to rise again,
Or stay beneath, contented with death.

17

Mother, keep your hands on the plough.
Study the stars for signs and songs.
Keep away from the thalassic trader,
Away from his vessel and gunpowder.

Guard your borders and be bothered by unusual winds.
Dance when aroused by wine,
The trance thereafter enjoy.
Set forth and set sail in your own vessel.

Write your sights and handshakes afar.
Leave me nothing but a chest-load of papyrus.

Sub-surface Condition

1

In my sleep I float
Near sooted chimneys
And smell smoke rising
From the mass
Of idle bodies, from the hooves
Of roaming nomads
Kicking and stomping
Through this land.

In the callus hands
Of a life I once lived,
Cradled, I smell the crisp rise
Of smoke, an ascendance
Becoming me leaving
The scale of memory,
Leaving this shell
That cocoons me

From where waters run
Against stones,
Upstream, washing
Up against my umbilical chord
Buried between shrubs
Where weeds spring,
Waiting for dawn-dew
That never comes,

For sunlight obscured by August clouds.

2

In this colossal space,
Curled up between posts,
My bed and I,
The panes bleed slimes
Of winter, dribbling
Down like okra whisked for effect.

I recoil between posts,
My bed and I,
As nothing here,
In this novel patch,
Equals the roast
Of corncobs at home.

3

It's threatening to snow,
And this greyness,
The utter blankness
Of haze and leafless trees
Removes me from me,
Layer after layer,
To where the marrows yield,
The shivers start,
And I rattle like gongs
In Ogume, the ancestral home
I cannot reclaim, that's now
A farfetched note I pluck
For effect.

4

The flakes are visible from here.
God must be at work.
The spaces without are rather concealed
And made dark by the utter whiteness
Of grains descending in place
Of rain.

God must be at work
As they say in a place I once lived,
Where the ritual of roosters at dawn,
The heroic leap of lizards from treetops,
Are God's fingers reaching down
To stroke our thighs.

5

A silhouette is taking shape
On my window pane,
The shape is sensual,
Surprisingly,
With smooth lines,
Suggestively,
Arousing curves
I could not have conjured
Without those fingers that descend
To stroke my thighs.

Descent

1

The city flutters like the sashes
Of a dress, diagonal lines,
Vertical lines, zigzagging

As we confine ourselves to this cask,
Stranded in the company of strangers,
Some too young for the silence we share,

Too old for a quick chatter,
For the station-stop voice
Before the snub,

Before we hit the cobbled core,
Left to inhale the burdened air
Cold as the pages of time,

Our senses sharpened
By the shuffle of shoes,
The casual click of lenses

Snapping rows of brick
Shrouded in time.

2

In the confines of this coach,
We lose ourselves.
We die and come alive,

Sniff ourselves, dissolve as the bus beeps,
As the doors fold
And spit us into the cold void.

A column of bodies, straight as careless strokes,
We plod down the city aisle,
Our novelties borne on our breasts,

Our gazes aslant as we descend
Into the catacombs.

3

The city wafts,
Held in a jar,
In a senseless pulse

Of traffic,
A sublime trap
That rushes

As dusk descends
In doses, as the bus beeps
And the doors fold

To release us
Into a waiting storm
That'll dissolve us
Into the coming night.

4

I see the image in his eyes,
Love unsure, bare, his face marked
By what the windowed traveler,

Entranced by passing cars,
Cannot know: the resolved resent
Lovers keep to their breasts,

A marsupium of coal
That burns but left to thrive,
Left to flare

Until the embers die
And the heart, shrunken, palpitates
With new sets of veins.

5

And winter is the story of a pail
Dipped in a hole, where it hits
A hard end, without heroic return
With bustling brims;

A child swaddled in wool,
A kin's skull hooded to the ear,
Hands crossed from breast to breast,
Bleeding feet at journey's end ...

6

As the new one here, there are things
You need to know.

Once, in a winter like this,
We set sail for temperate climes
In search of the perfect sun.

Ignore distant dates.
But picture this:
Blokes in the belly of boats,

The trampoline bounce
Of the sea uneasing full bellies,
A hundred barrels of booze for them

To belly when the going gets rough,
To toughen them against conscience,
The orgasmic shiver of noble flags

Raping neutral winds,
A fact you must read up
And be merry at the names you meet,

Names I cannot say for fear of visitation.
So we set sail in search of warmth,
Nothing more, nothing less.

Alas, and as you may have heard,
Tents were pitched and names were named.
Maps were made and soon, in haste,
Business began.

So tell me, my friend,
What is it like where you come from?
From the way you shake

To this whip of wind,
I can tell you've come a long way.
Another bloke in a boat?

Will you pitch tent here?
The maps are drawn, my friend,
The boundaries tight to the neck.

You don't stand a chance, my friend.
What do I know!
I have seen the world tip in favor of beggars.

As it is Elsewhere

A symphony, inundating varieties
That upturn my narrow scale
Of preference, leaving me drained
From bottom up, calling, tugging
My sleeves at dawn. At dusk I am
In a labyrinth that leads nowhere.

This menu before me – a mouthful
For my spice-proof tongue.
Eclecticism adrift. Music, food, souls –
New and distant – calling, tugging
My sleeves at dawn. At dusk I am
In a labyrinth that leads nowhere.

The highways are highways that run
From here to there, uninterrupted
By political dance. Coherent zigzags,
These highways that run me into a daze,
Calling and tugging my sleeves at dawn.
At dusk I am in a labyrinth that leads
                        nowhere.

A kaleidoscope, of disagreeing forces,
A pot of wax and wood, fleetingly solid
As departures from here to there,
Everywhere, calling and tuggging my sleeves
At dawn, and at dusk I am in a labyrinth
That leads nowhere, running myself into a daze,
                        a race that leads nowhere.

Lost Voice

In this sorted trench,
The air cuts your voice,
Excluding you
From rooftop screams.
But before this –
Mirroring mirage,
Coating brown
With pale blue hue,
And the outrage
Of the new you
Away from home –
You were loud
As madness,
Authenticity
In form and flesh,
You bled life,
Sour style cut loose.
But now, like them before you,
You wax dry, lifeless
In a pool
Of shielded lights.

Displacement

I pinch my lobes for steps but hear thuds
in the murky yonder,
where you cut a meek shape in the dark.

Without you pillows are props for tears.
The blue walls mock my surficial scratch,
as I stroke my yoke

in this cube, vast air, this cube without you,
where cobwebs clutter memory,
and life twice the pain

of displacement

Cassava

Our days on earth are like grass; like wildflowers, we bloom and die.
 —Psalm 103:15, NLT

1

If you're reading this now, dear friend,
Downloaded to your phone, held up
To your face, wherever you are,
On a plane home, (you asked, I declined,
Preferring this frost to that free ride),
 wherever you are,
As confessed before you left,
I've lost interest in these cuts on my wrist,
That I carry with me, collected from years
Of peeling cassavas day and night,
Peeling with razor-sharp knives
That slipped and sank their fangs
 into my flesh.

The cassava mound is a mass of roots.
Each root, or tuber as some say,
Is uniquely shaped, in brown shades.
A mound is sometimes high, hundreds of roots,
Side by side, waiting to go through
 our razor-sharp knives.

Our razor-sharp knives,
With which we peel for two nights
 each week,
Attacking the mound from all sides,
Picking each tuber like ants racing grains
To a hole, ants, picking from all sides
 until the mound gives
Leaving behind its scale,
Like shavings of wood, coiled up in shapes
Made by our blades.

2

Uprooted from the earth, like we all are,
Extensions of worms, cassavas come smeared
               in mud
And our fingers, holding them,
Will stink of sap and dirt.
But that's the start, as the real stench comes
               when the peeling is done
At which we bring out plastic tubs, fill them
With water, throw the tubers in
To wash and haul them
               into plastic drums,
Four to five drums filled
               to the brim,
Covered with their lids, and left
To ferment for days, until a stench like death
Rises from each drum.
The stronger that smell, the more we know
How dead they are
               down there,
Entombed in their own slime,
               down there,
Mushy, rotten, starved of air.

We humiliate them more
By exhuming them from each drum,
Lumping them in tubs again,
And calling the Grinder man whose job
Is to go from block to block
Grinding cassavas,
               already fermented,
Into near-smooth pastes.

He arrives, our grinder man
Whose machine stands on two wheels,
Dragged between blocks, from stop to stop
To the port of call.
He tops the fuel on his beast
               mounted on a two-wheel cart.

The Grinder's beast sits on a two-wheel cart,
                two tires
                between
A chassis so old it grates.
A Lister engine in front,
A funnel-shaped grinder-box at the back,
A space between both.
A belt runs from Lister to box.

As the beast roars and empties smoke
                into the air,
The belt propels the grater
That chops cassavas into near-smooth paste,
Excreting that paste into a waiting tub
Underneath the funnel-shaped box
                between the wheels.

And from the tub we scoop
And transfer to waiting drums.

When the Grinder leaves,
We close the drums and leave to "bathe,"
A weak attempt to clear the stench
                from our pores, our hairs;
A weak move, for our buckets
                of water
From which we scoop and splash
Are not enough and what's the point
When a day or two
We go back to that stench,
To the drums of near-smooth pastes
To "wash" and bag.

To "wash" is to send those pastes,
                against their wish,
To square contraptions,
Sifters placed on tubs.
                A sifter,
A simple, near-blind net, like mosquito nets,
Hemmed on all four sides,
Framed in, on all four sides
By wood, a square sift.
                And so we scoop,

Three plate-sizes per time,
Into the sift, and mix the mush
               with water,
Rocking our palms back and forth, "washing"
The cassava paste, washing and sweating
Until venous strands, alone, remain
On the heaven-ward side of the sift;
Underneath, in the tub, pure pulp waits
To be scooped into sacks.

When the sacks are tied, they sag, bulky,
Clumsy, dripping starch,
As we lump them on a palette,
Cover them with tarpaulin,
And pile heavy rocks on them to drain
               the last drop of juice.
And off we go to "bathe,"
A weak attempt to cleanse the stench
               from our pores,
Where they lodge against our will,
Trailing us to school, in our pores,
Driving us mad, in our pores.
A weak attempt to cleanse, for a day or two
We return to those sacks where pastes,
Now thick as dough,
               lie.

3

    When we return to re-mix the "dough,"
    It is to lighten the thickness of the dough
    By adding water, cup after cup, kneading,
    And re-entering the "new" dough in small
                    non-sacks,
    Then we break and try again to "bathe"
                    the stench away,
    For the night at least, for at dawn, before the sun
                    appears,
    The market-runner will come with his truck.

              With his help,
    The runner whose truck stinks of stale sap,
    We haul the bags away, to market stands,
    Where middlemen from restaurants
    Will come to bid for each bag, after which
    Wheelbarrow-men are called, and the bags are
    Wheeled to waiting vans, to kitchens away.
    Where, emptied and re-processed,
    They end up in flat plates,
    Served in stench-free chunks,
    With *Egusi* or *Ogbono* soup,
    With pints of beer to drive them home.

    And so it ends, the miserable lives of cassavas,
    Perhaps a metaphor for our own lives.

    But we don't end up in clean plates,
    Rid of the smell in our pores.
    Instead we re-do the loop,
    Picking tubers from the mound,
    Attacking the mound from all sides
                  like ants
    Picking grains of salt off the floor,
                  like ants . . .

A Small Experiment

As a child, I had the habit
Of trailing ants as they hauled grains
Of salt across the kitchen.

I'd watch them pass the grain
From ant to ant,
Careful not to drop it in dirt.

They'd march in a single file,
Covering ant-miles
In a human blink.

The last to hold the grain
Would place it on a pile,
And then back for another grain.

One day I began to wonder
What they'd taste like,
Those little workers.

Would there be blood
If I bit a head?
Would the rest mourn and cuss?

I turned to see
If I was being watched.
Then I stooped.

They dropped the grain of salt.
The line stood still,
Perhaps waiting for a sign.

I moved an inch,
They fled from me.
I pinned one down with my thumb,

Picked and squeezed hard
Between my fingers.
It neither screamed nor struggled,

But silently disappeared
Between my teeth.
I waited for flavors to ooze.

My taste buds died.
The rest stood away from me.

And I could tell,
From how they formed a semi-circle
Away from me,

That they knew what I had done.

Supplication

I don't know what costume to wear,
What color-mix asplash my face,
Adrip my chest, will send chills
Down their spines.

But I know the pang of thirst, the fang
Of malaria on bare flesh,
The pain of protests, lunatics in Cadillacs.

And I've seen the dead on all fours,
And know an itch as old as death.
I know a child in Kru town
Poisoned by its mother's milk,
Left to defend itself.

I've had my share, and ask to wear
Life around my neck, to share the stench
Of rotten flesh, the sting
Of recurrent nightmares.

May I wear what I know
Around my neck, memory, this life,
A gift from the quarry, a pendant
Hammered out of shape
By life, the elements
And time, concealed in earth's sackcloth.

I'll wear them around my neck
And on my wrists, to frighten the world
With what I know and own from birth.

From Cradle to Puzzles

Before the world walked through my mind,
Stripping it of all layers of trust,
Life was an epic quest, sunrise a marvel,
A luscious leaf left to life.

The future was a tiny dot, a fascinating pore
On life's backside. I lived by the second,
And thoughts were steps
Outside the gray margins of logic.

Time was neither named, nor a piece
Of ticking device. But a set of routines.
Second thoughts came with age,
The passing of bleak birthdays.

Fear came with knowing that shards cut
When picked, and tea – slurped in haste – burns.
Slammed with knowledge, I replaced colored spaces
With packs of required puzzles.

Kru Child

Kru child.
Barefoot in a pond of grass,
Strutting round the sour-sour tree,
Whistling to the chirp of weaverbirds.

Child of the tropical sea,
Wreathed in leaves of glee,
Fishing with a revolting worm
On a lone hook.

Kru child, bold and beautiful,
Glowing in the West African sun.
White teeth, as the morning
That divides night from dawn.

Son of uncommon powers,
Silent at dusk and alert at dawn.
Daughter of the full moon,
Braided hair smooth as eel.

The whirlwind was here.
It tore through Kru town,
Rattling hutments of zinc and wood.
But Mama fed you greens.

And Papa paddled to safety
In the grim silence of night,
Dodging the glittering flight
Of bullets.

Now the soothing sea breeze blows.
You yawn and stretch.
Pepper-soup is served,
Straight from rested hearths.

But you must watch where the sail goes,
For the peace that hangs is neither
Here nor there, a caged cobra
That fattens itself.

Above a Postwar Town

Hovering above ground,
I see roofless shacks smiling,
open cracks that reveal deep cuts
healed but bleeding; doors and faces
that lead to wandering minds
murdered by sights of blood.

I see shoulders, broad and narrow,
hurting from years hauling rags,
poor slender stalks holding heads
twice large by lack, protuberant veins
thumbing mothers to death;
a toddler slurping trickling milk . . .

Between streets and parches
of shrubs, life stretches out on bare back,
beaten to pulp by human torrents.
And behind cotton trees the slain stand
where shallow graves show skulls
begging to age in peace.

But peace is ten tents away,
in projector slides planted
away from streets where teens,
weaned from guns, group for booze,
heading nowhere, waiting for glimmers
of escape from this tomb.

Boy in Transition

Blank eyes in shock.
Nose running to meet drawn lips.
Neck tiny and veined-out-loud.
Belly shooting, sagging
On a beaded waist.

Rationed supplies are carted
For darting skeletons maneuvering
Between death, blankets,
Between pills, condensed milk in cans.
For his running orifices green leaves are napkins.

Tangos are to Kalashnikovs.
And there are headlines to deal:
Big boots pounding,
Big shots fleeing,
Bush paths crowded,

His lights go out.
His eyes refocus to see,
A panoramic view, the carnage.
In this altered state peace is death,
To die is to see from a vantage point.

Notes to Note

I see a set of blinking eyes
On the other side of the bamboo fence,
Bright between bamboo stems.

They are watching me play a piece
On a keyboard dead but kept alive
By AAs lined in a wooden box.

A misplaced chord, an odd touch,
And I'm Chopin in this silent space,
Exuding airs I lack but none can tell.

They nod and tap and giggle along,
Then clap as I rush to keep the tune.
Words are spurn to match my sound

And they are on key,
Stomping their fragile feet,
Noting the pretentious pound of my fingers.

Transition

He shared the air with ten inmates,
Their broad chests heaving in the metallic heat
Of that Liberian jail.

There were ten bars between him and the rest of us,
His innocence a debris left to the claws
Of passing ghosts.

Death hovered like bees waiting to sting.
He held his breath, courted peace,
And was released to the waiting void.

Now he floats above ground,
A veil between him and the rest of us.

On a Bamboo Shelf

His first Bokowski was picked
From a pile of damp books
On Broad Street,

Tranströmer and Sontag
In a worn issue of *Antaeus*
Fished off a corner,

Hauled to Robertsport,
Away from Broad Street.

It stormed that night.
His thatched roof had prominent gaps.
Tranströmer and Sontag were served raindrops
And fragments of dismembered reed.

He placed *Antaeus* on a ledge outside,
Near the hen house where his friend's corpse
Was later dumped for two days,

Embalmed in fresh grass and ash.

Holes Filled with Mud

When time is of age
And there is nothing more to learn,
I will peel from this shield
Of degradable matter,
And coagulate you
Into a mass of letters.

You, who once littered my crevices
But now return, in shocking jolts:
The descent of whips on my back,
The stare of empty dinner plates,
The floor with holes filled with mud ...

You, a copy of that riddled past,
You return in fragments of shock,
Washing up against the present,
Begging for fame at all costs.

A Whisper, A Chime

1

Between my fingers I hold your hair,
Its textures our lair to prowl.
The *Imo* covers me as I teach you to leap
Without a glance. Stuttering,
Laughter between steps,
You brace to start anew,
And become me in skin and soul.

Maneuvering the dense/dark
Of the Cape Mount, swimming
In the shallow mouth of the Piso,
We become one again:
Gazelles on a hill, a village of birds
On a deciduous tree.

2

I recall how we drowned in jars
Of wine tapped from nearby trees.
We plunged without care,

Gulping until our senses were sore,
Wrenched from us.
Piso washed up at the door,

Pushing back plastic bags,
Rocking pegged boats.
Bug bites tethered your neck

Like beads,
Your lower back collecting its share
Of tropical tan.

3

I recall the flirtation
Of a broad-chested dancer,
Who thought you tourist

And I your guide.
But my voice,
A whisper then a chime,

Halted his advance in midstride.
So he danced with another,
With whom he trudged home

After dark.
Atop a bamboo bed,
Coiled up like worms,

We studied the stars
Through thatched roof gaps,
And drifted to orchestral crickets.

4

The streams on our palms run
Aslant.
Mine, on the left,

Are confluences nipped taut
Between thumb
And index.

Yours are more rivers than streams.
Interpretations are subjective.
The palmist does his pocket a favor.

Gunpowder

Held down
By shivering grips,
Immobilized

By the physicality
Of transient
Hormonal flights.

Firm nerves alert,
Neck veins alert,
Hot tears in shuteyes,

Words slurred
In pulsations,
In whispers.

An inevitable plunge,
One could say.
Night against youth,

One could a say.
An upward progress,
Rummaging through

For exhaustion,
Until pleasure,
A nightly ritual,

Enters the warmth
Of death as sleep symbolic
Of a hyperbolic drift

Beyond logistics –
Uniting for the making
Of flesh from mud.

Then the sudden end,
Of which memory will parody,
Adding absent glitters.

The final huzzah,
Cataclysmic or not,
Is neither relief nor redemption

But a premature leap
Of instinct, the detonation
Of caged gunpowder.

A Pinch to the Skin

The question was a single line:
Where to hear the call
Of silence in corners at night.
Their replies came in hues,
Tumbling in tangents
And metaphors askance
But of a kind that returns,
After a glance or two,
To the center from where
It began: the flap of feathers
On a dying bird,
Tossed against a coming wind,
The grating sound
Of old shutters against
A coming cold,
The sedate laughter
Of pointed heels
On cobbled curbs
(The street perforated in the aftermath),
The spasmodic kick
Of legs losing blood
To the click of guns and cameras . . .

These and more in hues of sorts,
Answers, improvisations,
Exempli gratia:
The cry of Moorman's bow on a Paik-made cello,
The cryptic groan of strings on television,
The wail of willing fingers distending
The bounds of performance.
Or, I improvise here:
The bow as saw hacking through
Historical strings
Holding down idle torsos,
The wail a violent liberation from life listless
And austere.

The question was a single line.
And down came answers in gusts:
The sensual appeal
Of a forked path
Through a meadow,
A lung-full of air drawn to ease the run;

The fragile dance
Of newly hatched chicks,
The wobble on ridged ground,
The attempt at flight,
The run for defenseless bugs,
The concomitant joy . . .
That instinctual quest;

The colorless droop
Of weeping willows,
Wrinkled and bald by weather,
Hope obscured or don't judge the future
By an absence of lush;

The instagrammed cover
Of conflagrations,
The sky a splintered sheet
Of falling hope;

Evanescence or the past as absent;
The chink of light upon a stage,
Upon the liquored dance
Of drunk gatekeepers,
Their guns dusted and cartridged;

Excision or that lump in your throat,
The pointless fear
Of a hooded approach;

Color or the disgust
In pronouncing that word,
Repulsion in etymology.

Color: to conceal, to cover;

Blee, the comfort of ignoring how words evolve,
The privilege of repertoire without a flinch,
Without a pinch to the skin.

Acknowledgments

I am grateful to the editors of *Numero Cinq, Blue Rock Review, the 2010 Arvon International Poetry Anthology, Kin Poetry Journal,* and *Mad Swirl,* where some of these poems, in various forms, appeared for the first time.

Timothy Ogene was born in Nigeria, but has since lived in Liberia, Germany, the US, and the UK. His poems and stories have appeared in *Numero Cinq, One Throne Magazine, Poetry Quarterly, Tahoma Literary Review, The Missing Slate, Stirring, Kin Poetry Journal, Mad Swirl, Blue Rock Review, aaduna*, and other places. He holds a first degree in English and History from St. Edward's University, and a Master's in World Literatures in English from the University of Oxford. His first novel, *The Day Ends Like any Day*, is scheduled for publication in April 2017. He lives in Boston.